D1320999

*With love,*
*Papa* x

# BEAR GRYLLS

LION

A Lion Book
an imprint of
**Lion Hudson plc**
Wilkinson House, Jordan Hill Road,
Oxford OX2 8DR, England
www.lionhudson.com
ISBN 978 0 7459 5501 8
Distributed by:
UK: Marston Book Services, PO Box 269, Abingdon, Oxon, OX14 4YN
USA: Trafalgar Square Publishing, 814 N. Franklin Street, Chicago, IL 60610
USA: Christian Market: Kregel Publications, PO Box 2607, Grand Rapids, MI 49501
First edition 2009
10 9 8 7 6 5 4 3 2 1 0

**Acknowledgments**
pp. 17, 20, 46: scripture quotations taken from the *Holy Bible, New International Version*, copyright
© 1973, 1978, 1984 International Bible Society. Used by permission of Zondervan and Hodder &
Stoughton Limited. All rights reserved. The 'NIV' and 'New International Version' trademarks are
registered in the United States Patent and Trademark Office by International Bible Society. Use of either
trademark requires the permission of International Bible Society. UK trademark number 1448790.
p. 11: scripture taken from the *New Century Version®*. Copyright © 2005 by Thomas Nelson, Inc.
Used by permission. All rights reserved.
p. 15: Scripture taken from *The New King James Version* copyright © 1982, 1979 by Thomas Nelson, Inc.
pp. 41, 59, 64: scripture quotations are taken from the *Holy Bible, New Living Translation*, copyright ©
1996. Used by permission of Tyndale House Publishers, Inc., Wheaton, Illinois 60189. All rights reserved.

A catalogue record for this book is available from the British Library
Typeset in Photina MT
Printed and bound in China

To my sons, the great joy in my life.

This little book is a culmination of all that I have learnt about the game of life.

I have learnt these simple truths through many mistakes and many falls. I have learnt them from watching and being around those that I love and admire, and I have learnt them through the hard times that life sometimes throws at us.

I have also learnt that what I value most about life is found close at home; just being with you three boys and your Mama.

I hope these simple truths help you blossom in the game of life and I hope they help you follow your hearts and many dreams. I hope they remind you to cherish those close to you, and to live life boldly and with a smile.

You are the most wonderful joy in both our lives, and I could never have imagined such good fortune to be able to hold you close to me so often (although it never seems enough!)

I adore you and am oh, so proud of you.
You are the best.

With love, Papa x

Aim to live a wild, generous, full, exciting life – blessing those around you and seeing the good in all.

Follow your dreams –
they are God-given.

Have a few close friends who
you see often – their friendship
matters more than having
many shallow acquaintances.

Be honest and vulnerable
with those close to you.
It creates strong bonds.

'I think I'm addicted
to chocolate'

'me too'

'and girls'

'me too'

Don't be held back, either by fear or by lack of confidence. Go for it, despite these very normal emotions that we all feel occasionally.

# Build people up.

❧

Be faithful –
any old slime can
cheat!

# Smile and laugh more than is considered normal!

Be loyal – it is the mark of a man.

Remember the verse:
'We are the sweet smell of Christ among those who are being saved and among those who are being lost.'

2 Corinthians 2:15

Exercise at least every other day – make it a habit. Then you will shine even brighter.

Choose your job carefully – do work that excites you. It is where you will spend so much of your time.

Don't be afraid to be
weak occasionally.

# Choose a job that betters people's lives.

Snack on nuts and fruit – they suppress appetite and make you strong!

Remember the verse:
'I can do all things through Christ who strengthens me.'

Philippians 4:13

Cheerfulness under adversity
is a key character trait in
the game of life.

Moments of doubt are part of life. Accept them and remember that Jesus himself said: 'My power is made perfect in weakness.'

2 Corinthians 12:9

'Thank you, your majesty'

Nobility is not a birthright – how we act in the big moments defines who we are.

Encourage, encourage;
help, help.

Remember this verse by heart:
'Even there your hand will guide me,
your right hand will hold me fast.'

Psalm 139:10

⚜

Understand that failure is an essential
stepping stone on the road to success.

'OK, so this puddle
is to be avoided next time'

Always keep the big picture in mind – you are greatly loved by Jesus and your job is to love him and others in return. The rest is detail.

'That's a big picture'

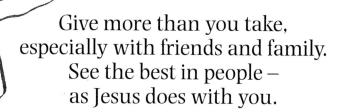

'one for me,
two for you'

Give more than you take,
especially with friends and family.
See the best in people –
as Jesus does with you.

✤

Compliment people –
kind words
can change lives,
and people rarely forget.

# Manners really matter, in fact they maketh the man.

Remember that how you speak
about others speaks
loudest about yourself.

If you want to see the real man –
give him power over people and
see what he does. Remember this
in how you treat people.

Be the most enthusiastic
person you know!

❦

Love Jesus.

❦

Find a fun, honest,
down-to-earth local church
and support it.

'Come on Dad'

# Be gentle.

Consider others better
than yourself.

⚜

Be especially kind,
thoughtful and generous
to those who are
overlooked in life – this is
the measure of a
real man.

Pray to Jesus daily
– what a person
he is to have
helping you!

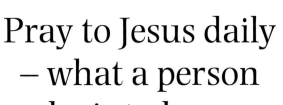

Be courageous
in key
moments.

Eat lots of fruit and veg –
they fight all the free radicals
that try to slow you down.

# Be kind to those whom others neglect.

If supply is short then look for something to give away. It is a law of the universe – to receive you must first give.

Put ten per cent of your income aside and give that money to those in need – whether friends or charities. You have the power to save lives.

Speak generously about people.

Sometimes it is worth losing a battle
to win the war.

Jesus came to seek and to save us –
let him do his job!

Help friends in need.

Don't lend money;
rather, give it.

Say 'why not?'
rather than 'why?'

Generally in life, try to leave things five minutes too early rather than five minutes too late.

The people to be nicest to in life are your wife and your children – give them the most time, energy, and love and you will be happy.

Spend more time with your family and less at work – no one on their deathbed says they wish they had spent more time in the office!

# Marry only for love.

This is a cracker to remember:
'And be sure of this: I am with you always,
even to the end of the age' (Matthew 28:20).
I had this engraved on Mama's wedding ring
when we married!

# Lead by example.

'walk
this
way,
please'

No one cares how much you know until they
know how much you care.

❧

# Don't lie.

You have two ears and one mouth – use them in proportion: listen twice as much as you speak!

Don't better people's stories.

'But remember the Lord your God,
for it is he who gives you the ability to
produce wealth' (Deuteronomy 8:18).
So, thank God for your many blessings
then go out there and blossom!
It is okay to succeed!

Always look people in the eye.

# Have a firm handshake.

When you ring someone, first ask them if it is a good time to talk.

❧

Don't be afraid to be quiet and let others shine.

Treat others as you would like to be treated.

Be extra cautious if mixing
business with friendship.

Pride comes before a fall – so let others win.
There is room for everyone to do well!

Be ambitious – think big and take calculated risks.

Be open, honest and fair
in all your dealings.

It is okay to be weak – with less of you
there is more room for God.

When you're right, shut up,
and when you're wrong, admit it.

Many great people over the centuries have depended on their faith – it is a sign of great strength to need Jesus in your life.

# Be the first to apologize.

Enjoy the silence.

Make a little time to be quiet
by yourself every day
and just be.

Don't go to battle unless
it is absolutely necessary –
to turn the other cheek takes
great strength and courage.

'Here's my other cheek!'

Crying is healthy!

✤

Always hold hands with those you love
whenever you have the chance.

✤

Gratitude, gratitude, gratitude.

Relax. You have no need for the common concerns of life. Remember Isaiah: 'The Lord will guide you continually' (Isaiah 58:11).

Don't worry about anything that is outside of your sphere of influence – if you can't change it, don't waste time worrying about it!

Learn a few clean jokes and a good card trick.

Laugh at yourself.

# Learn to play an instrument.

Swim in streams!
Be spontaneous – it's fun!

❖

# Watch a sunrise
# occasionally.

Bet your life on Jesus.
Ultimately that's the big one!

❖

Make people smile every day.

Know that I love you and
am always with you and
am oh, so proud.

Your Papa xxx

The Lord himself
watches over you!
Psalm 121:5